What people are s

DARE TO ~~L~~

THE KIDS

'I would recommend it to my friends if they were feeling like they needed a confidence boost, for sure!'

Freddie aged 11

'*Dare to Be You* has really helped me get rid of my own inner doubts and I am sure it will help you.'

Oliver aged 13

'This book is GREAT. It has really helped me to understand that it is OK to be different and will really help me when I go back to school.'

Toppsta reader aged 8

'I read it with my mum and she loved it too and said it helped her a lot. It is written by Matthew Syed who is a champion table tennis player, so it uses his own childhood and growing up as examples. Some of the examples of what has happened are REALLY funny like the tracksuit and his dad's car.'

Toppsta reader aged 8

'I thought it was good that it was written in chapters and some parts of it were really funny. This book has loads of interesting facts in it and lots of science. I am going to read it again and again and I am going to "Dare to Be Me!'

Toppsta reader aged 11

'I love this book so much! I read *You Are Awesome*, which was great, so I knew this one wouldn't disappoint me.'

Toppsta reader aged 11

THE ADULTS

'We have read *Dare to Be You* with our youngest child, who has quite severe dyslexia. This causes him to often have low self-esteem, and this book, very much like *You Are Awesome*, allows him to see the very best in himself and to know and acknowledge that there is no such thing as normal. It's been incredibly empowering for him, and also a great tool for us as parents.'

Giles Paley-Phillips

'A very inspirational book packed with excellent quotations and references to REAL people that both children and adults can relate to. The comedy is spot on and had me laughing out loud at times.'

Toppsta teacher reviewer

'Thank you Matthew Syed for such an inspiring and honest book!'

Toppsta teacher reviewer

'Matthew Syed has done it again! I wish we had had books like this when I was younger.'

Toppsta teacher reviewer

'A really motivating, well-written book about embracing differences and being yourself. This is perfect for Key Stage 2 and I'll definitely be sharing it with my year 4 class.'

Toppsta teacher reviewer

THE MEDIA

'Charming, informative and inspiring motivational book for children.'

The Times

'Matthew Syed's first book for children, *You Are Awesome*, was a massive hit. This is the sequel and we reckon it's just as good, if not better. With lively text, stylish illustrations and real-life examples, it sets out to encourage young readers to build their confidence and resilience and follow their own path in life.'

The Independent

'Hugely inspiring.'

Press Association

For Rita and Andy. The best of teachers.

First published in Great Britain in 2021 by Wren & Rook

ISBN: 978 1 5263 6314 5
10 9 8 7 6 5 4 3 2 1

Wren & Rook
An imprint of
Hachette Children's Group
Part of Hodder and Stoughton
Carmelite House
50 Victoria Embankment
London EC4Y 0DZ

An Hachette UK Company
www.hachette.co.uk
www.hachettechildrens.co.uk

Publishing Director: Debbie Foy
Managing Editor: Liza Miller
Senior Editor: Sadie Smith
Consultants: Kathy Weeks and Angharad Rudkin
Art Director: Laura Hambleton
Designed by Kathryn Slack

Additional images supplied by Shutterstock
Additional artworks by Ollie Mann

Printed and bound in the United Kingdom

Matthew Syed

The Dare TO BE YOU Journal

ILLUSTRATED BY

Toby Triumph & Ollie Mann

wren
&rook

CONTENTS

INTRODUCTION

On the first night it was me, David, Tom, Stephen, Craig and Ash.
And it was weird. All these new guys. In **MY** house.

It had all started when my dad applied for a new job. It was a big
promotion. Working in the government department responsible for tea,
coffee and bananas (yes, this is a thing). He bought a new suit for the
interview and wore a tie with bananas on it that he had found in my
grandad's wardrobe. I thought the tie was a bad idea, but it seemed
to go down better than I expected and he came back from the
interview with a brand-new job in banana management.

Which meant that the family had to move to London.

BUT. THIS WAS SERIOUSLY BAD TIMING FOR ME.

I was coming to the end of secondary school and my table tennis was
just starting to get pretty serious. I had made the national team for the
first time and had a brilliant coach who was really pushing me hard. I just
couldn't leave for London. Not then. My whole **LIFE** was in Reading.
I stopped eating bananas in protest, but it did no good. My dad decided
to rent the house to students and a date was set for the big move.

DISASTER.

That was until I managed to get Peter Charters (my table tennis coach)
to convince my mum to convince my dad (I know, stick with me …)
to let me stay at home in Reading. With Peter checking in on me now and

again to make sure that I wasn't just living off Haribos and only having a shower every third Tuesday.

So, that is how I came to be living with David, Tom, Stephen, Craig and Ash. In my own house. Now, you are probably wondering by now whether there is a point to any of this. And I promise that there is. I am getting to it. Right now.

You see, this new arrangement with me living with five students was a big change. I didn't have my mum around anymore to cook my dinner and my dad wasn't around to talk to after I'd lost a big match. I even missed my brother (don't tell him that though). And I had to get used to this totally new set up while five total strangers moved into my house.

That first night, **Kid Doubt** was there. Enjoying every minute. Delighted to see how nervous I was. Wishing I would say stupid things when I introduced myself to these guys.

Now I should probably check here that you know **Kid Doubt**? You must do? You've read *Dare to Be You,* right? Great. You are awesome. (No, wait … that's the other book). SKIP THIS IF YOU HAVE READ *DARE TO BE YOU.* WHAAAAAT? You haven't read it yet? I'll get over it (probably) but I'll just need to give you a little spoiler about what is in it. You see, I introduce you to **Kid Doubt** in *Dare to Be You.* He (or she, everyone has their own **Kid Doubt)** is that voice in your head that holds you back. The one who creates the nagging doubts in your mind that you are not quite good enough. **Kid Doubt** can make you feel insecure. Make you do things you are not proud of. And most importantly, stop you doing some of the things that you would really like to do. *Dare to Be You* is about ignoring **Kid Doubt** and silencing that voice in your head.

9

Anyway, back to it. Me, David, Tom, Stephen, Craig and Ash. Oh, and **Kid Doubt**.

Now, it might sound like we must have had some kind of seven-bedroom luxury mansion. But nothing could be further from the truth. My dad, keen on a money-making scheme, was all for packing our three-and-a-half bedroom house as full of as many paying students as he possibly could. I was surprised when he didn't rent out the family bathroom.

Tom had the lounge. Craig had the dining room. Not ideal as they didn't really have a proper door between them. Me, Stephen and Ash had the three bedrooms. And David had the half-sized bedroom, which was so small that the Syed family had previously decided it wasn't big enough for our pet hamster.

But this experience taught me so many things. I realized that I could change a lightbulb and even warm a sausage roll in the microwave. And even though my mum wasn't in the same house with me, she was always on the other end of the phone and I could call her day or night if I had a problem. The change didn't seem so huge after all. But even more than that, I realized how very different people are. None of the five guys were anything like me. **AT ALL.**

AND NONE OF THEM HAD THE SLIGHTEST INTEREST IN TABLE TENNIS.

Craig was interested in philosophy and talking about the big questions of life, like 'how can I be sure that I am thinking?' David was constantly irritated with Craig at the start. He couldn't understand the point of these questions. To be honest, David was just irritated generally. I think he was struggling to sleep standing up. (There wasn't really room for a proper bed in that half-sized bedroom.)

Tom didn't seem to understand the idea of sharing. He ate four of my frozen pizzas before I realized that he was doing it. Ash spent 19 full minutes cleaning his teeth in the morning. Locked in the family bathroom, flossing away while the rest of us queued up downstairs outside the single toilet. I couldn't understand how he could be so selfish.

And still no one was interested in table tennis. At all.

But here is the thing. I grew to love living in that house with my new housemates. They were all different to anything I had ever known and they showed me how useful it can be to see things from a different perspective. (It turned out that Ash needed the full 19 minutes because he had some false teeth after a bad hockey accident.) I realised that not everyone was obsessed with hitting a small white ball across a net. And I understood that people had different strengths and different weaknesses.

In the end we arranged a rota for all the boring cleaning and cooking stuff. Everyone did their bit. We had brilliantly interesting chats in the evenings about all kinds of topics and I learned so much about the world from those guys. And (I think) they liked me too.

Right. I think we are ready to get to work. Ready to find the confidence we need to follow our own path. But before we begin it is worth remembering:

1 We are all different. Very different. And we can learn so much from people who think differently to us.

2 You have a lot to offer. We need to silence **Kid Doubt**, be brave and do the things that are right for us. Even if that means your path is a little bit different to someone else's.

3 If you have a question related to banana management, my dad is definitely your man.

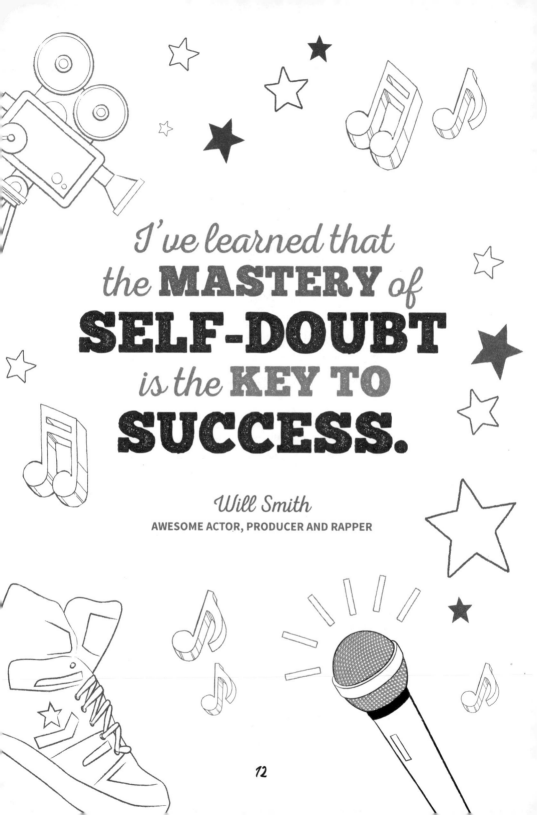

I've learned that the **MASTERY** of **SELF-DOUBT** is the **KEY TO** **SUCCESS.**

Will Smith
AWESOME ACTOR, PRODUCER AND RAPPER

DEFYING KID DOUBT

One of the worst things our **Kid Doubt** can do is make us feel like we're the only ones feeling insecure. But you are not alone. Even superstars have had their struggles with **Kid Doubt** – and won!

DAVID BOWIE

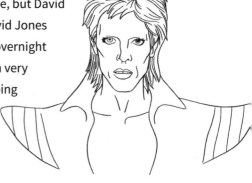

He might have been a million-record-selling musician with adoring fans worldwide, but David Bowie started out as a boy called David Jones from Brixton, London. He wasn't an overnight success, and in fact, he suffered from very low self-esteem. But Bowie wasn't going to let his **Kid Doubt** get in his way. He reinvented himself as Ziggy Stardust and followed his own path to become a global superstar.

SERENA WILLIAMS

She might have won 23 grand slams and four Olympic gold medals, but that doesn't mean that tennis ace Serena Williams doesn't struggle with doubt. She's looked up to by millions of people around the world, but as a child Serena wasn't confident in herself. She spent her childhood wanting to be just like her big sister Venus, even ordering the same food as Venus in restaurants. It took Serena a long time to feel comfortable being herself, but once she did, there was no stopping her.

TOM HANKS

His career spans 40 years, and he's done it all: won two Oscars, become a Hollywood A-lister and voiced everyone's favourite cowboy, Sheriff Woody. But even to this day, the veteran actor Tom Hanks questions his own abilities. His **Kid Doubt** makes him worry that he's a fraud who's no good at acting and he's going to lose everything he's worked so hard to achieve. But Tom knows that he can't let his fears win. He says that sometimes you just have to fake your confidence until it returns.

ZOË SUGG

With millions of followers online telling her on a daily basis how wonderful she is, you'd think Zoë Sugg would have the confidence of a superstar. But all the supportive likes and comments in the world can't stop **Kid Doubt** creeping in. There are times when Zoella (that's her YouTube name) second-guesses herself and doubts the decisions she's making in her life. And while she's not always sure how to silence her **Kid Doubt,** she knows that talking about it always helps. Remember, no matter what our life looks like on social media, it doesn't always tell the real story. Everyone has days when they question themselves.

KID DOUBT FIBS

Now we know that even superstars have had to face off **Kid Doubt**, try researching some of your own personal heroes to find out what insecurities they have had to face. Write down the best example here to always remind yourself that you're not alone.

MATTHEW'S HERO: *My dad (shhhh! Don't tell him. It will just go to his head)*

FIBS KID DOUBT HAS TOLD THEM:
My dad moved to England from Pakistan when he was just 22. His Kid Doubt told him all kinds of things when he arrived. That he might not make any new friends in this new country. That he might not fit in ... and he proved Kid Doubt wrong!

MY HERO IS:
....

FIBS KID DOUBT HAS TOLD THEM:
....
....

We often...don't feel inherently **GOOD ENOUGH** *or* **SMART ENOUGH** *or* **WORTHY ENOUGH.** *You are worthy because you are* **BORN** *and because you* **ARE HERE.**

Oprah Winfrey
INSPIRING ENTREPRENEUR, CEO, PRESENTER AND ACTOR

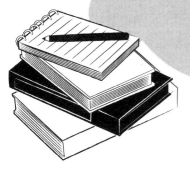

MEET YOUR KID DOUBT

Now we know about other people's **Kid Doubt**, it's time to look in the mirror and confront yours. What are some of the unhelpful things that your **Kid Doubt** tells you that you know in your heart not to be true? Write these in the speech bubbles below.

Next, show your **Kid Doubt** that you don't have time for their lies and negativity by writing down some confidence-boosting comebacks.

Who defines "cool", anyway?!

My friends do like me, and they like me for who I am!

WHEN **KID DOUBT** COMES CALLING!

My best friend Emma had a swimming-pool party for her birthday. Massive problem. Everyone else could swim really well and I ... well, I couldn't. You know how a fish thrashes around wildly if it is taken out of the water? Well, that's exactly how I looked when I was **IN** the water. **Kid Doubt** was telling me that everyone would laugh. So I didn't go. Emma was so disappointed. And I didn't get a piece of the *Star Wars* cake we had both been looking forward to.

SO, WHAT COULD I DO DIFFERENTLY?

Well, I could find out some more details beforehand and plan ahead. If there's a shallow end of the pool, I could hang out there, be honest with my friends and tell them I'm not a strong swimmer yet. If that isn't an option, I could sit at the side of the pool and cheer everyone on. At least I'd get the cake afterwards and it's better than sitting at home. Note to self: practise swimming so I look less like a fish out of water **IN** the water.

Think of the times that **Kid Doubt** got in your way and what you could have done differently. Write these down in the boxes opposite, and hold on to these thoughts for the next time **Kid Doubt** comes calling!

WHEN KID DOUBT CAME CALLING:

· ·

· ·

IF THIS HAPPENED AGAIN, I'D...

· ·

· ·

WHEN KID DOUBT CAME CALLING:

· ·

· ·

IF THIS HAPPENED AGAIN, I'D...

· ·

· ·

WHEN KID DOUBT CAME CALLING:

· ·

· ·

IF THIS HAPPENED AGAIN, I'D...

· ·

· ·

ACHIEVEMENT
ALBUM

My brother had a brilliant idea. (It only happened this one time, so let's not give him TOO much credit.) While we were playing table tennis, he started something called the **Achievement Albums.**

He started a book that catalogued our (well, mostly HIS to be honest – I only got the occasional mention) successes. When we (again, mainly HE) did something we were proud of or when we handled a difficult problem really well, he would record it in the album.

To start with, I couldn't really see the point of this, but quite quickly we had several of these Achievement Albums. These albums were a treasury of positivity. They reminded us that we'd done some pretty great things, and that if we had done them before, then we could go out and do them again.

HOW ABOUT MAKING AN ACHIEVEMENT ALBUM OF YOUR OWN?

Every time you do something you're really proud of, no matter how big or small – whether listening to a friend with a problem or doing well in a test – record it in your album. You can include a photo if you like. The next time **Kid Doubt** comes knocking and you're struggling to remember some of the great things you have done, open up the album. You'll be amazed by how full it is and all the awesome things that are in there.

UNDER PRESSURE

I know, I know. It's all well and good me sitting here telling you not to listen to **Kid Doubt**, but he's a pretty convincing guy. And he is SUCH a hanger-on. Always turning up when other people are trying to convince you to do something that you're unsure about.

Here are some useful tips to help you stand your ground and keep **Kid Doubt** quiet:

O Go with your gut. If something doesn't feel right for you, even if your friends are okay with it, don't join in.

O Don't be afraid to say 'no', even to your friends. Good friends will respect your decision.

O Support other friends if they're being encouraged to do something that they're not happy about.

O If all else fails, walk away from the situation and find something else to do with other friends.

O If your 'friends' keep trying to make you do things you're not happy with, it could be time to find some new friends who feel the same way as you do.

O If things are getting dangerous, never hesitate to go and get help from an adult.

PEER PRESSURE +
KID DOUBT
=
ONE BIG PRESSURE POT

The good news is that it gets easier to stand up for yourself the more you practise it! Rope in a friend or family member and, using the tips, act out these situations to get comfortable with standing your ground.

PRESSURE POT 1: You've promised to help your mum clear out the garage on Saturday, but your friends want you to hang out with them instead. They're suggesting you lie to your parents by claiming you've got a school project to work on. **Kid Doubt** thinks this is a great idea, but you know this isn't the right thing to do. How do you turn your friends down?

PRESSURE POT 2: Your friends are suggesting you skip choir practice and go shopping with them instead. **Kid Doubt** thinks you should go with them, but you know it's wrong and not worth all the trouble. What do you say?

PRESSURE POT 3: You really like Sam, but your other 'friends' want to ditch them and hang out without them. You know this will really upset Sam, and even though **Kid Doubt** is telling you Sam will get over it, your gut is telling you it's mean. How do you stick up for Sam?

THE **WORRY** CLOCK

Did you know that some researchers think that people spend nearly two hours worrying **EVERY SINGLE DAY**? Just imagine all the things you could be doing with your time instead! Try a little experiment: for the next week, write down one thing that **Kid Doubt** has said to you in the 'Worry Clock' below. (Note that it doesn't have to be *every* day.)

Sunday — WHAT'S THE WORRY?

Monday — WHAT'S THE WORRY?

Tuesday — WHAT'S THE WORRY?

Wednesday — WHAT'S THE WORRY?

Thursday — WHAT'S THE WORRY?

Friday — WHAT'S THE WORRY?

Saturday — WHAT'S THE WORRY?

Now, I bet you can think of something better to do with your time than worry. It's time to turn those minutes spent worrying into something fun, or something you've always wanted to try. Draw or write down some ideas at the bottom of the hourglass, then note down your favourite at the end.

MONDAY´S WORRY
TUESDAY´S WORRY
WEDNESDAY´S WORRY
THURSDAY´S WORRY
FRIDAY´S WORRY
SATURDAY´S WORRY
SUNDAY´S WORRY

Next week, instead of worrying, I'm going to ...

THE MANIFESTO MAKER

In *Dare to Be You* (a mega book apparently, J.K. Rowling can't stop calling me up to tell me she wishes she had written it. Oh wait! I think I dreamt that), I talk about the plan I came up with when I knew that I needed to face down **Kid Doubt** and get good at daring to be **ME**. It was like a manifesto (aka a plan) for being, well, me.

MANIFESTO:
A written statement declaring your BELIEFS, AIMS or GOALS

At times, when things got confusing and I wasn't sure what to do, I would go back to the plan and it would remind me of the things that were important to **ME**. It's been a huge help and I use it **ALL** the time.

It made me think that **YOU** might find it helpful to have a plan (aka a manifesto) of your own. Let's work on it together through this journal, step by step, until, before you know it, you've got your own tailor-made manifesto at the end of the book.

For the first point in your manifesto, think back over all the activities you've done in this chapter and decide which bit helped you the most. What advice or activity did you relate to more than anything else, something that you'd always like to remember, especially when things are hard? It can be more than one thing. Remember: it's **YOUR** manifesto, so make it flexible to suit you.

MANIFESTO MAKER

Things I've learnt to help me beat Kid Doubt:

○ ○

○ ○

○ ○

○ ○

Amazing! You've just written the first point in your manifesto.

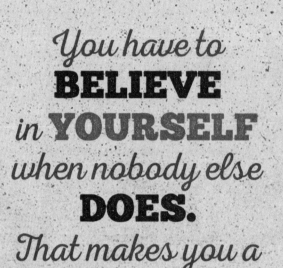

You have to **BELIEVE** in *YOURSELF* *when nobody else* **DOES.** *That makes you a* **WINNER** **RIGHT THERE.**

Venus Williams

FANTASTIC FORMER WORLD NUMBER 1 TENNIS CHAMPION

NO MORE AVERAGE

Have you ever thought, 'I just want to be normal' or 'I just want to be like everybody else'? Well, guess what? Big news! Everything is CHANGING on that front.

BECAUSE THE FUTURE IS ALL ABOUT YOU.

You see, in the past so many things (what we should eat, medical treatments, furniture) were all designed for the 'average' or 'normal' person. But the truth is that very few people are exactly the same as the 'average'. This means that there's loads of things out there that don't work for lots of people. Take smartphones for example. The average screen size is 14 centimetres, which fits really well in the larger hand of the 'average' male. But women typically have smaller hands than men, so whilst they make up 49 per cent of the population, most smartphones are too large for lots of women to use comfortably.

No matter how alike people seem at first glance, look a bit closer and you will realise that we're all incredibly different and unique. But as the world changes, and technology improves, we can tailor things to work best for each person individually. Which means what you wear, what you eat, what medicine you need, what you watch on TV… it's all going to be just right for **YOU**.

No more average. No more normal. So, there is no more point in trying to fit in. We don't need to anymore!

Can you think of some other examples of things that have been designed with the average person in mind? Things that might not work for you if you are a little bit different? Think about a particular design fail that you have noticed, and then get creative and design a new, **BETTER** version and sketch it in the box below.

BELIEVE IN YOURSELF

We've all had friends, parents or teachers say things about us that don't seem fair. You know the sort of thing: 'Why can't you be more like your sister?' or 'Don't let him have a go, he'll be rubbish at it!'. The problem is that sometimes these comments can get to us. Get inside our heads. And we can start to believe that they might be true.

Has this ever happened to you? Can you think of a time when someone has said something unkind to you or unfairly compared you to someone else? Let's take back control and write down why this comment was untrue or unfair. Don't let other people's opinions of you become your opinion of yourself. Remember: you're **unique** and **brilliant** just the way you are!

I've done the first two for you:

I WAS COMPARED TO …
My brother at table tennis

I'M DIFFERENT FOR LOTS OF GREAT REASONS, INCLUDING … *He is two years older than I am, so has had two years more to train.*

PEOPLE DON'T THINK I'M VERY GOOD AT ...
Cooking

WHAT THEY DON'T KNOW IS ...
I have bought a recipe book for beginners and am practising. I actually don't mind too much if I'm not Gordon Ramsey because I am better than Gordon is at table tennis and I love table tennis.

SEEING THINGS DIFFERENTLY

Not everyone sees things the same way; what might be obvious to you can completely pass someone else by. All sorts of things can influence the way we look at things, including our education, where we were brought up and our family values. Look at the **optical illusions** on these pages, what do you see? Then try them out on your friends. Does anyone come up with different answers to you?

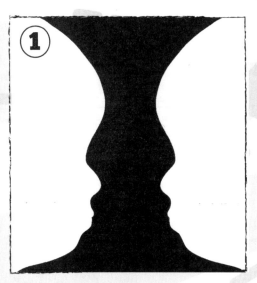

I see:

○ ● ○ ○ ● ○ ○ ○ ● ○ ○ ○ ● ○ ○ ○ ● ○ ○ ○ ○ ○ ● ○

My friends see:

○ ● ○ ○ ○ ● ○ ○ ○ ○ ○ ● ○ ○ ○ ○ ● ○ ○ ○ ○ ● ○

○ ● ○ ○ ○ ● ○ ○ ○ ○ ● ○ ○ ○ ○ ● ○ ○ ○ ● ○ ○ ○

I see:

○ ○ ● ○ ○ ○ ○ ○ ● ○ ○ ○ ○ ○ ● ○ ○ ○ ○ ● ○ ○ ○

My friends see:

○ ○ ● ○ ○ ○ ○ ● ○ ○ ○ ○ ○ ● ○ ○ ○ ○ ○ ● ○ ○ ○

○ ● ○ ○ ○ ● ○ ○ ○ ○ ○ ● ○ ○ ○ ● ○ ○ ○ ○ ● ○ ○

I see:

· · ○ · ○ · ○ ○ ○ ○ · ○ ○ ○ · ○ ○ · · ○ · ○

My friends see:

· · · ○ · ○ · ○ ○ ○ · ○ ○ ○ · ○ ○ · ○ ○ · · ·

· · ○ · ○ · ○ ○ ○ · ○ · ○ ○ ○ · ○ ○ · · ○ · ○

MANIFESTO MAKER

Remember our manifesto? Well, it's time to write your second point.

When I'm worried about fitting in and being 'normal', I'm going to remember:

· · ○ · ○ ○ · ○ ○ ○ ○ · ○ · ○ ○ ○ · ○ ○ ○ · ○ · ○ ○ · ○

· · ○ · ○ ○ · ○ · ○ ○ ○ · ○ ○ · ○ ○ · ○ · ○ ○ ○ · ○

· · ○ · ○ ○ ○ · ○ ○ ○ · ○ ○ ○ · ○ ○ · ○ ○ · ○ ○ ○ · ○

· · ○ · ○ ○ ○ · ○ ○ ○ · ○ ○ · ○ ○ · ○ ○ · ○ ○ · ○

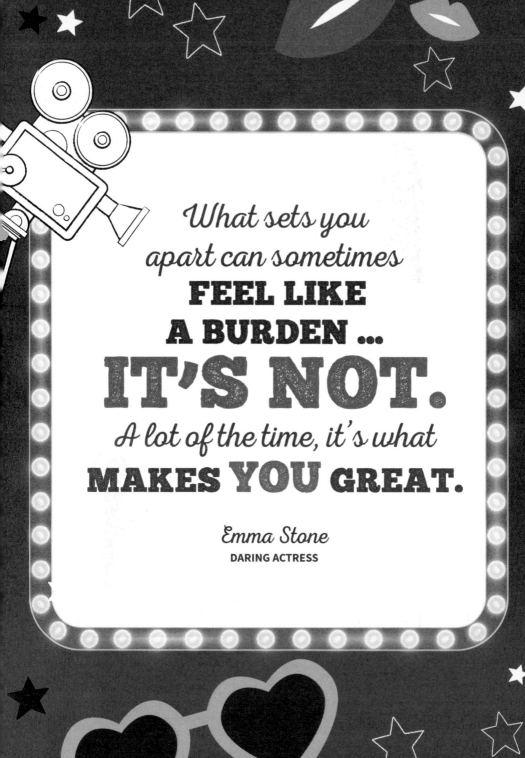

What sets you apart can sometimes **FEEL LIKE A BURDEN ... IT'S NOT.** A lot of the time, it's what **MAKES YOU GREAT.**

Emma Stone
DARING ACTRESS

BEING DIFFERENT

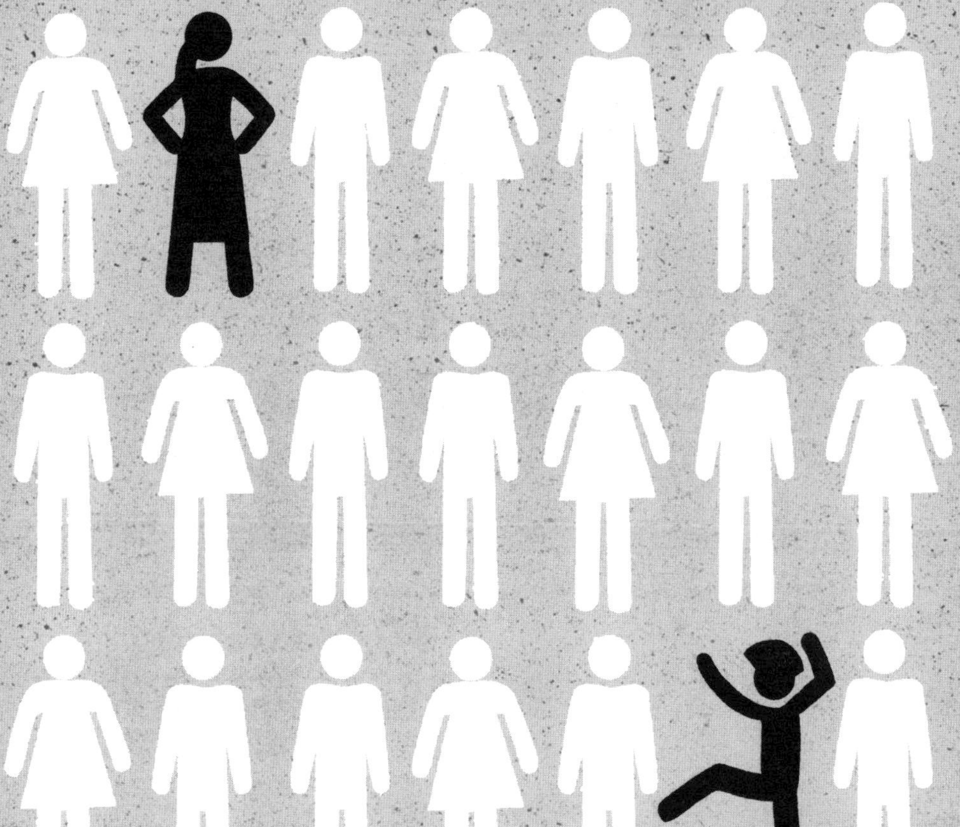

MAKES THE BIGGEST DIFFERENCE

SAFETY NET

Have you ever thought about what it must feel like to be a tightrope walker? Well, me neither actually. But it must be quite an odd job, trying to get everything right while everyone is staring at you. This is why most tightrope walkers have a safety net below them! Nerves are wobble-inducing.

Do you recognize that feeling? Everyone looking (some wanting you to fail or to laugh at you) and just wanting to be **ANYWHERE** else but there? Like any time my mum picked me up from school in our car. It's a long story, but the car had the words 'SYED BROTHERS' emblazed in orange on the side – it was a massive metal embarrassment on wheels.

It's never fun when you feel like this, but sometimes these things happen, and it's important to have someone (your version of a safety net) to turn to; someone you can talk to about what happened. They won't always be able to fix the problem, but they'll be there to listen and act as a 'sounding board' on the situation. You can also build yourself an action plan for when you feel a little **TOO** different.

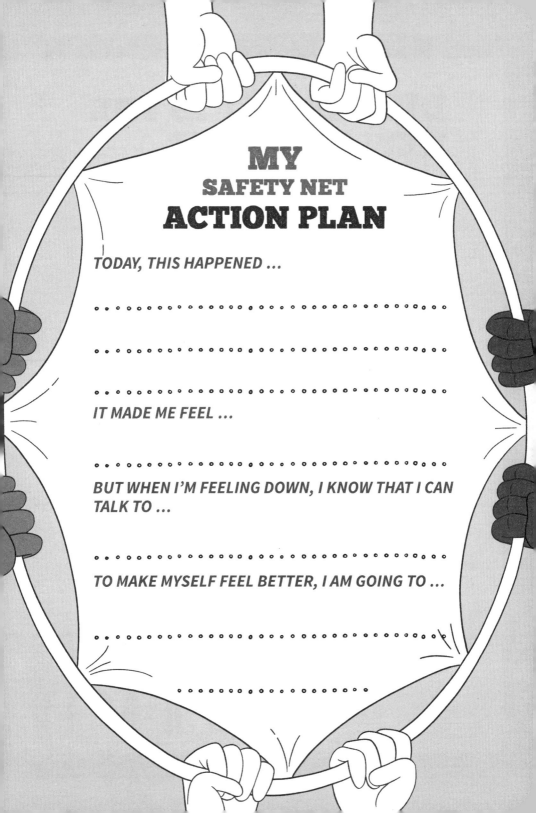

MY
SAFETY NET
ACTION PLAN

TODAY, THIS HAPPENED ...

· ·

· ·

· ·

IT MADE ME FEEL ...

· ·

BUT WHEN I'M FEELING DOWN, I KNOW THAT I CAN TALK TO ...

· ·

TO MAKE MYSELF FEEL BETTER, I AM GOING TO ...

· ·

· ·

DIFFERENT IS THE NEW AWESOME

When we're feeling self-conscious and like we'll never fit in, sometimes the best thing to do can be to look around for inspiration. Is there anyone you look up to who has embraced their **DIFFERENCES**? Who is comfortable in their own skin and happily shows that in everything they do?

Draw or stick in pictures of people who you think are awesomely different and owning it, and the next time you're feeling unsure, come back to these pages for a confidence boost. You might like to add some of their inspirational quotes, too.

MY "DIFFERENT IS THE NEW AWESOME" CHAMPIONS ARE . . .

MAKE LEMONADE

Have you ever heard the phrase 'when life gives you lemons, make lemonade'? It's all about trying to turn a negative into a positive. (Lemons are of course sour, but you can turn things around by making delicious sweet lemonade from them!) An optimistic attitude to life can make all the difference.

Beyoncé loves this phrase. She was even inspired to call her album *Lemonade* because of it! Even the fabulous Queen B suffers insecurities and setbacks now and again, but she works hard to turn those into something positive.

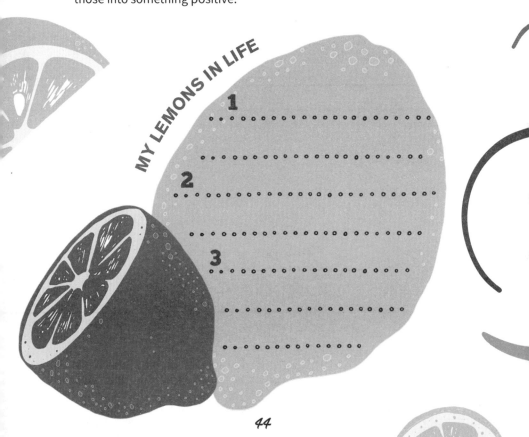

MY LEMONS IN LIFE

1

2

3

Sometimes we wish we could change things about ourselves – we might wish we were taller, better at sport, have the ability to crack funnier jokes – but there's always a positive to make out of a negative, even if we can't see it at first.

List your 'lemons' in life – the things you'd rather change – and then think creatively about how to turn them into positives and make lemonade …

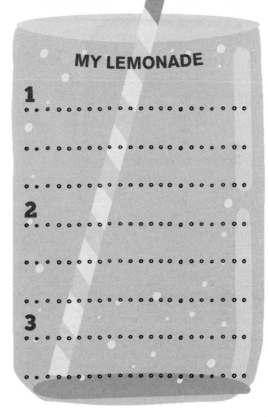

MY LEMONADE

1 ⋯⋯⋯⋯⋯⋯⋯⋯⋯⋯⋯⋯

⋯⋯⋯⋯⋯⋯⋯⋯⋯⋯⋯⋯

⋯⋯⋯⋯⋯⋯⋯⋯⋯⋯⋯⋯

2 ⋯⋯⋯⋯⋯⋯⋯⋯⋯⋯⋯⋯

⋯⋯⋯⋯⋯⋯⋯⋯⋯⋯⋯⋯

⋯⋯⋯⋯⋯⋯⋯⋯⋯⋯⋯⋯

3 ⋯⋯⋯⋯⋯⋯⋯⋯⋯⋯⋯⋯

⋯⋯⋯⋯⋯⋯⋯⋯⋯⋯⋯⋯

SQUAD GOALS

If someone asked you to put together the perfect team for a school project, who would you choose? Would you be tempted to pick your closest friends? The thing is, the best teams are often made up of people who think differently to each other. If you and your friends are all really similar, then you'll probably only look at things from one point of view. But if you have a wider variety of people on your team, there'd be no stopping you. Create your own dream team by assigning these roles to people.

The Comedian

They're always cheering everyone up with their jokes, but they're also good at noticing the little things that no one else considers (and usually making a joke about it!).

I'D PICK:

. . . .

. . . .

The Weight Lifter

They push everyone to work a little harder, and always encourage the team to make their ideas bigger and better.

. . . .

. . . .

WOULD BE PERFECT FOR THIS ROLE

The Scientist

They challenge everything, questioning ideas and making sure everyone can explain their reasoning.

THIS IS SO:

· · · · ∘ · · · · · · · · · · · · · · · · · · · ∘

· · · ∘ · ∘

· ∘

The Judge

They've got a really good moral compass, making sure everyone stays true to who they are and don't just follow the crowd. And if everyone's being indecisive, they'll always make a decision.

THIS SOUNDS JUST LIKE:

· ·

· ·

The Artist

They see things from a different angle to everyone else and consider things from many different viewpoints.

I'D CHOOSE:

· ·

· ·

· ·

MY TEAM ALSO NEEDS:

· · · · ∘ · · · · · · · · · · · · · · · · · · · ∘

· ∘

· ∘

YOU vs YOU

Change can be really hard to see and it is often so gradual that we don't notice it day-to-day. Think of yourself a year ago. How many more things do you know since then? Well, imagine life in five years' time, think of all the incredible skills and knowledge you'll have then! Write down all the things you've learned over the last year in the middle circle, and then dream big and put down all the new skills and knowledge you'll have in five years' time in the biggest circle.

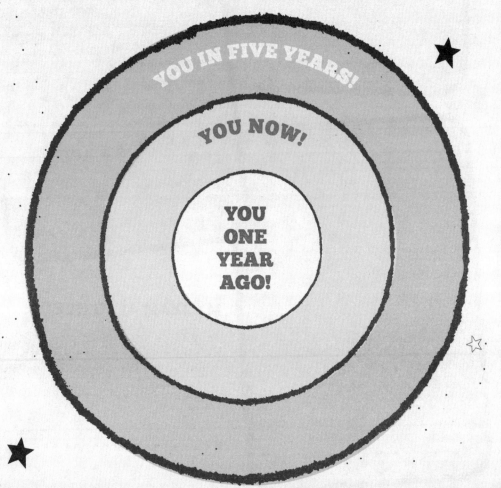

YOU IN FIVE YEARS!

YOU NOW!

YOU ONE YEAR AGO!

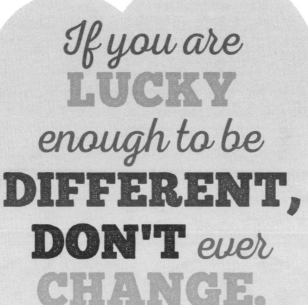

If you are **LUCKY** *enough to be* **DIFFERENT, DON'T** *ever* **CHANGE.**

Taylor Swift
FEARLESS POP SUPERSTAR

CHALK AND CHEESE

Me

Mark

Are you and your friends chalk and cheese or are you two peas in a pod? Some friends are so alike that people get them confused, but other friends can seem so different that people wonder how they get along. I thought me and my friend Mark were really similar, but when I looked closer, I realised we were actually quite different – and that's a good thing.

Pick a friend, think of ways that you're similar and put these in the gap where the circles overlap. Next, write down your differences in the other parts of the circle. Are you surprised by how alike or how different you are?

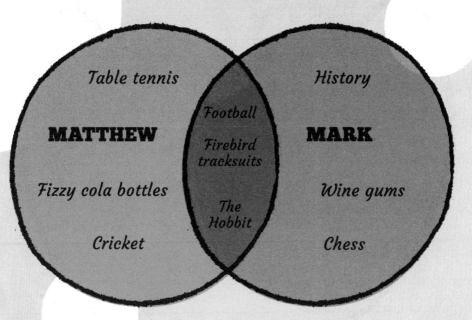

Table tennis

History

MATTHEW

Football

Firebird tracksuits

MARK

Fizzy cola bottles

Wine gums

The Hobbit

Cricket

Chess

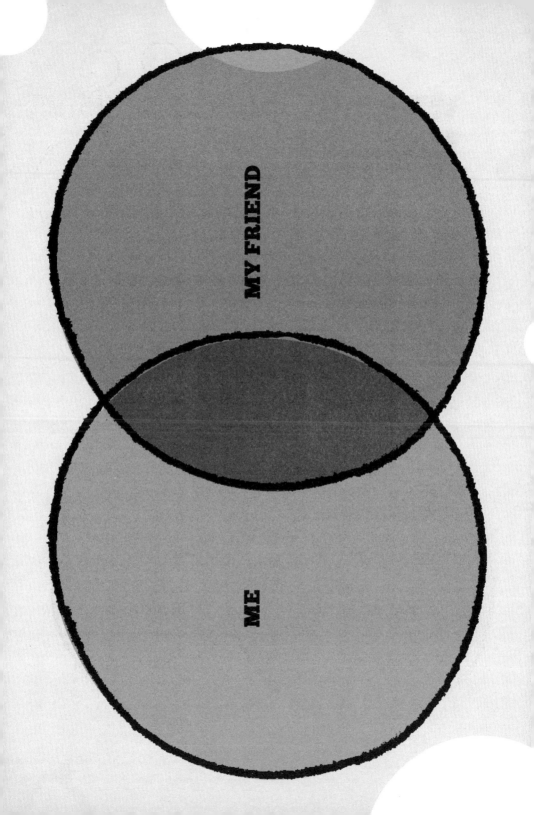

WANT TO WIN A NOBEL PRIZE?

Research has shown that you are more likely to win a Nobel Prize if you have a hobby outside your field of expertise. Amazing, right?! (But I must add that you do also need to be a world class expert in physics, chemistry or economics to win one of these things!) But why would having a hobby give you an even better chance? Well, it is because a hobby gives you a fresh perspective. It allows you to take in different ideas. Meet different people.

It's time to get some fresh perspectives. Think of a friend or family member you admire, but at the same time is different from you. Maybe they've got amazing artistic skills, while you can only master a stickman drawing? The more different they are, the better! Now, ask them some of life's big questions.

 **WHAT MOTIVATES YOU?**

. . . .

. . . .

WHAT DO YOU DO WHEN YOU'RE STUCK IN A RUT?

. . . .

. . . .

WHAT MAKES YOU HAPPY?

· · · ○

· · · ○

WHAT THINGS DO YOU IMAGINE YOURSELF DOING WHEN YOU'RE A GROWN-UP?

· · · ○

· · · ○

Next, go through their answers looking for clues. They might be different to you, but what have you learned from them that you could apply to your own life?

· · · ○

· · · ○

MANIFESTO MAKER

Manifesto time! What's the third point you'd like to add from things you've learned in this chapter?

When I get worried about being different, I'm going to remember ...

· · · ○

· · · ○

DON'T BE A CLONE

SPOT THE CLONE!

It's really easy to copy people we look up to. In fact, we do it without realising it! While copying some things about a person can be good – such as their hard work or their values – copying some other things can be pointless. It's important to keep it in check so we don't end up copying things that don't fit with **who we are**.

Draw or stick in some pictures of famous faces in the frames and think of some things about them that'd be good to copy – and what's probably best to leave to them! I have done the first one for you.

FAMOUS PERSON:
Kevin Keegan

GOOD TO COPY:
His dedicated training

THINGS TO LEAVE TO THEM:
Expensive cars etc. I don't have to buy everything that Kevin advertises just to be like him!

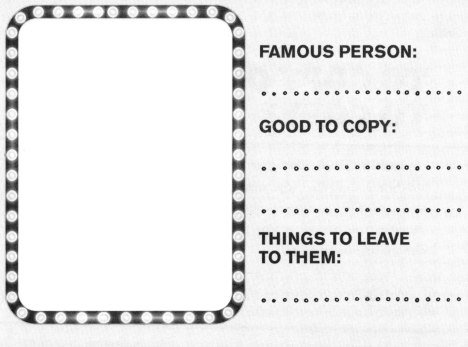

FAMOUS PERSON:

· ·

GOOD TO COPY:

· ·

· ·

**THINGS TO LEAVE
TO THEM:**

· ·

FAMOUS PERSON:

· ·

GOOD TO COPY:

· ·

· ·

**THINGS TO LEAVE
TO THEM:**

· · · · · · · · · · · · · · · · · · · ·

· · · · · · · · · · · · · · · · · · · ·

TO COPY OR NOT TO COPY?

How good are you at working out which behaviour is helpful to imitate and which you can probably ignore? Read the statements below and see if you can work out what could be helpful copying, and what could be over-copying, by matching them up with the answers opposite.

1 You've seen an advert on TV of your favourite actor selling the latest headphones. Should you rush out and buy them?

2 Jameela, the coolest person in school, has just taken up circus-skills classes. Should you start doing circus-skills classes as well, even though you have terrible balance?

3 You're off to the cinema with friends, but Chris turns up late and you all miss the start of the film. You're all really upset about it. Michael, your best friend, starts shouting at Chris. Do you start shouting as well?

4 It's School Sports Day and you're running the 800 metres. Every year, Jon does well in the race, and you know that he always trains ahead of Sports Day. You want to do well, too, so should you consider joining him on some training runs?

5 Ami always does well in tests, but everyone thinks she's boring because the weekend before a test she stays home to study and doesn't hang out with her friends. You've been getting low marks lately. Should you keep hanging out with your friends, or stay home to revise?

A Jon has got things sussed. If you want to improve any performance, practising and putting some work in always pays off. And maybe if you do some regular running ahead of School Sports Day, the race won't feel so hard on the day, either! But remember, it's not all about winning. It is also about doing the best that you can and enjoying it!

B It's always good to be open to new things, but if something isn't for you, don't try it just because your friend is doing it.

C Staying home once in a while to study is definitely the smart thing to do. Just think what the alternative could be – you could end up having to stay home more in the long run to make up for all the bad grades. Be more Ami. It could certainly help to improve your test scores.

D No. Just because someone else reacts in one way doesn't mean you need to copy them. Especially if how you feel is completely different.

E If you do need new headphones, check out if these ones are good and could suit **YOUR** needs. If you don't need any new kit, then don't buy them. Which headphones your favourite actor uses has nothing to do with how they just won that Oscar.

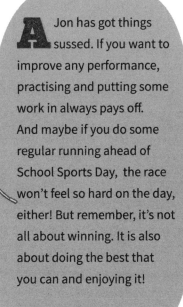

Answers: 1 = E; 2 = B; 3 = D; 4 = A; 5 = C.

When you're a child,
**ANYTHING AND
EVERYTHING
IS POSSIBLE.**
The challenge, so often,
is hanging on to that as we
GROW UP.

Dame Ellen MacArthur DBE
RECORD-BREAKING SAILOR

CHALLENGING CHANGES

BIO PHYSICS

MATHS

Change can be hard, but some people are better at dealing with it than others. Take this quiz to find out if you live for change, or you like things to stay just the way they are.

(1) You're moving house soon. This makes you feel:

A. Excited at the chance to make new friends.

B. A bit sad about leaving your bedroom behind.

C. Terrified. You refuse to go.

(2) Your swimming club is changing their practice from Tuesdays at 5pm to Thursdays at 6pm. How you do feel about this?

A. Tuesday, Thursday, you just want it to be Friday!

B. It'll be a bit weird not swimming on Tuesdays, but you'll get used to it.

C. You're going to give up swimming and look for a new thing to do on Tuesday nights.

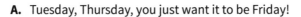

(3) You've grown out of your favourite running shoes and they don't sell that style any more. Do you:

A. Think it's awesome. Maybe a new style of running shoe will make you run even faster!

B. Give your old shoes a proper send-off and create a memorial for them in your room.

C. Stop running altogether. If you can't run in your old shoes, then you won't run at all.

(4) **Your favourite teacher is leaving school, and a new teacher is starting. What's your reaction?**

A. Sad, but you've had different teachers in the past and you remember that you were okay with that, so you'll cope fine with this change.

B. Give your teacher a leaving card and spend the weekend getting consolation cuddles off your mum and dad.

C. Vow to NEVER like the new teacher.

(5) **You always wanted to be a doctor, but you just found out that you need to be good at physics to study medicine, and that's your worst subject. Do you ...**

A. Refuse to dwell on your disappointment and instead, research similar jobs and find one that doesn't need a good grade in physics.

B. Sulk for a week.

C. Stop studying for your exams, what's the point if you can't be a doctor?

MOSTLY As

You're a cool cat when it comes to change. It can be tricky, but you take it in your stride. It's okay to feel worried about change sometimes though. Find someone to talk to if you're finding things hard.

MOSTLY Bs

You recognize how change can be hard, and sometimes you get a little dramatic about it (a 'shoe memorial'? Really?!), but you're good at dusting yourself off and trying something new.

MOSTLY Cs

You find change really hard and you like things just as they are. Remember to always talk to an adult when you're finding things hard and ask them any questions you might have about the changes. Lots of people find this stuff hard and that's OK.

Much of what I
STUMBLED
into by following my
CURIOSITY *and*
INTUITION
turned out to be
PRICELESS
later on.

Steve Jobs
CREATIVE GENIUS AND CO-FOUNDER OF APPLE

BUT WHY?

If you've ever spent time with a toddler, you know they ask '**WHY**?' a lot. They ask lots of (sometimes annoying!) questions because the world is still new to them and they're trying to understand it. Somewhere down the line, we stop asking 'why?' and often do things just because they're 'what you do'. Have you ever stopped to think about why you do certain things in your life or **WHY** you have certain goals? Well, let's do something exciting. Let's challenge them! I have done the first one for you ...

What's your favourite subject at school?

. . . .

. . . .

. . . .

. . . .

What are you doing this weekend?

PRACTISING TABLE TENNIS WITH MY BROTHER

WHY?

BECAUSE HE IS GOOD. BUT, HE LIKES TO ATTACK AND I PREFER TO DEFEND. MAYBE I COULD SEE IF SOMEONE ELSE AT THE CLUB COULD HELP ME WITH MY DEFENSIVE SHOTS?

WHY?

. . . .

. . . .

. . . .

. . . .

What's your favourite hobby?

WHY?

What activity would you love to try?

WHY?

What job would you like to have when you're older?

WHY?

Challenge yourself and get curious! Maybe you'll learn something new about yourself, or realise you need a change in direction.

GET QUIZZICAL

Ever wanted to know something but been too shy to ask, or has **Kid Doubt** ever told you you'd look like an idiot if you did? What questions have you been you afraid to ask in the past? Write them down and then decide on some strategies for finding the answers. **Kid Doubt** should not be holding us back from asking questions and broadening our horizons.

I WISH I'D ASKED MY TEACHER ...

TODAY, I ASKED ...

AND I FOUND OUT ...

I WISH I'D ASKED
MY FRIEND ...

I WISH I'D ASKED
MY PARENT ...

TODAY, I ASKED ...

TODAY, I ASKED ...

AND I FOUND OUT ...

AND I FOUND OUT ...

FIND YOUR VOICE

Everyone feels confused at some point or wants to challenge the way something is done. Whatever it is you're puzzled by – a task you're being asked to do or a lesson at school – it can be intimidating to ask questions, especially as **Kid Doubt** is normally lurking nearby. The thing is, it's **ALWAYS** okay to ask questions. Sometimes, however, it can take a little bit of work to make sure you get the answers you need.
Use these questions and tips to help clear things up.

WHAT'S THE ISSUE?

Tip: Narrowing down exactly what it is you're unsure about can help you describe your issue more clearly to others.

I'M PUZZLED BY . . . .

. . . .

REHEARSE WHAT YOU WANT TO SAY.

Tip: If you're worried you're going to forget what you want to ask, write your questions down on a piece of paper first.

MY QUESTION IS . . . .

. . . .

WHEN WILL YOU ASK YOUR QUESTION?

Tip: If you don't feel confident asking questions in front of lots of people, then choose a time when there are fewer people around.

I'M GOING TO ASK . . . .

. . . .

WHAT IF YOU STILL DON'T UNDERSTAND?

Tip: Sometimes people can misunderstand a question or give the same answer that you didn't understand the first time. Try phrasing your question in a different way.

I'M STILL UNSURE, SO I'M GOING TO . . . .

. . . .

THEY GOT CROSS AND DIDN'T ANSWER MY QUESTION.

Tip: Some people don't like being asked questions or aren't very good at answering them, but don't let that put you off. If one person isn't able to help you, find someone else you think could help.

**I'M GOING TO FIND THE ANSWERS
I NEED BY** . . . .

. . . .

CONNECTING THE DOTS

Whether it's moving house, changing school, getting poor grades or just working out the settings on the new TV, we all have to deal with changes and difficulties. These can be scary, but I bet there's loads of times you've dealt with similar things in the past – you just haven't connected the dots.

It's not always obvious how things are connected, but writing them down in this way can really help you to remember how a problem was solved or how a big change turned out okay in the end.

ACHIEVEMENT
Write down achievements that you're really proud of, no matter how big or small.

ACHIEVEMENT

. . . .

. . . .

. . . .

ACHIEVEMENT

. . . .

. . . .

. . . .

ACHIEVEMENT

I won a table-tennis trophy after practicing really hard.

ACHIEVEMENT

I made some new friends when I moved up a year at school.

THE ISSUE

I keep failing science tests.

THE ISSUE
Think of some changes or problems you're finding difficult at the moment.

THE ISSUE

My brother is moving up to secondary school and I'm still at primary school.

THE ISSUE

. . . .

. . . .

. . . .

THE ISSUE

. . . .

. . . .

. . . .

WHAT'S THE MISSING LINK?:
Can you connect things you learned from your past achievements to current difficulties to help solve them?

MISSING LINK

. . . .

. . . .

. . . .

MISSING LINK

Use my table-tennis practise timetable as a template for my study.

MISSING LINK

. . . .

. . . .

. . . .

MISSING LINK

I've learned how to do things without support in the past. I bet I will be okay without him!

TO CHANGE
OR
NOT TO
CHANGE?

It can be hard to makes changes in your life. We can't change everything, but we **CAN** change some things to help make our lives a little easier or achieve our goals quicker. Fill in the grid opposite to help you to understand the things you can and can't control in your life. I've given some examples to get you started.

WHAT CAN I DEFINITELY CHANGE?

What I eat for breakfast each morning.

To practise my table tennis four times a week instead of three.

· · · · · · · · · · · · · · · · ·

· · · · · · · · · · · · · · · · ·

· · · · · · · · · · · · · · · · ·

· · · · · · · · · · · · · · · · ·

· · · · · · · · · · · · · · · · ·

· · · · · · · · · · · · · · · · ·

· · · · · · · · · · · · · · · · ·

· · · · · · · · · · · · · · · · ·

WHAT DO I THINK I CAN'T CHANGE, BUT MAYBE IF I'M BRAVE ENOUGH TO QUESTION IT, I CAN?

My mum really wants me to play the piano. I really want to play the guitar instead. I wonder if she will mind?

Whether I really want to hang out with kids that tease me for reading *The Hobbit*. I mean, are they really my friends?

· · · · · · · · · · · · · · · · ·

· · · · · · · · · · · · · · · · ·

· · · · · · · · · · · · · · · · ·

· · · · · · · · · · · · · · · · ·

· · · · · · · · · · · · · · · · ·

· · · · · · · · · · · · · · · · ·

WHAT CAN I DEFINITELY NOT CHANGE?

The car. The one with 'SYED BROTHERS' painted in massive orange writing on the side. Yes, that one.

Something unkind someone said to me yesterday at school (although I can change how much I let it affect me).

· · · · · · · · · · · · · · · · ·

· · · · · · · · · · · · · · · · ·

· · · · · · · · · · · · · · · · ·

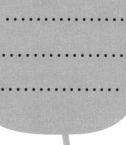

· · · · · · · · · · · · · · · · ·

· · · · · · · · · · · · · · · · ·

FUTURE FANTASTIC

The world is changing every day. There are jobs that used to exist that simply don't any more. Did you know that before the invention of a machine, an actual person used to line up the pins at the end of the lane at a ten-pin bowling alley? And, there are jobs that don't exist today that will do in the future. Can you think of some awesome jobs that **MIGHT** actually exist one day? Draw your ideas in the boxes below and give them a job title!

Someone who has to look after all the robots that have taken over a lot of the jobs that people used to do.

JOB TITLE:
Robot Wrangler

Turning everyone's waste into amazing new inventions.

JOB TITLE:
Rubbish Designer

JOB DESCRIPTION:

JOB TITLE:

JOB DESCRIPTION:

JOB TITLE:

JOB DESCRIPTION:

JOB TITLE:

CHANGE

will **NOT** come if
we wait for some
OTHER PERSON
or if we wait for
SOME TIME.

WE *are the* ONES *we've*
been **WAITING FOR.**

WE *are the* CHANGE
that **WE SEEK.**

Barack Obama

FORMER US PRESIDENT AND CONSTANT CHANGE-MAKER

PROBLEM SOLVED!

When you come across a problem in life you have two options. You can:

A) HOPE THAT SOMEONE ELSE WILL FIX IT

OR

B) BE YOUR OWN ACTION HERO AND SORT IT OUT YOURSELF!

Small actions can often be enough to make your world a better place. Sometimes we just have to think creatively about a solution and not let **Kid Doubt** fool us into thinking it isn't a good idea.
What do they know, anyway?!

Time for you to practise your problem-solving skills! Think of a couple of challenges you have come up against recently and brainstorm some solutions. I have done the first one for you …

STEP 1: WHAT'S THE CURRENT ISSUE AND WHY IS IT A PROBLEM?

I have maths and English homework to do on the same night that I have football practise, so I just don't get enough time to do my homework well!

STEP 2: WHAT'S A SOLUTION THAT WOULD IMPROVE THIS SITUATION?

An extra day to do my maths homework would really help me out here.

STEP 3: HOW WILL YOU ACT ON THAT SOLUTION AND MAKE IT HAPPEN?

Ask my teacher if I can get my homework done a day early or hand it in a day late. Surely they would want me to do it well rather than have to rush it?

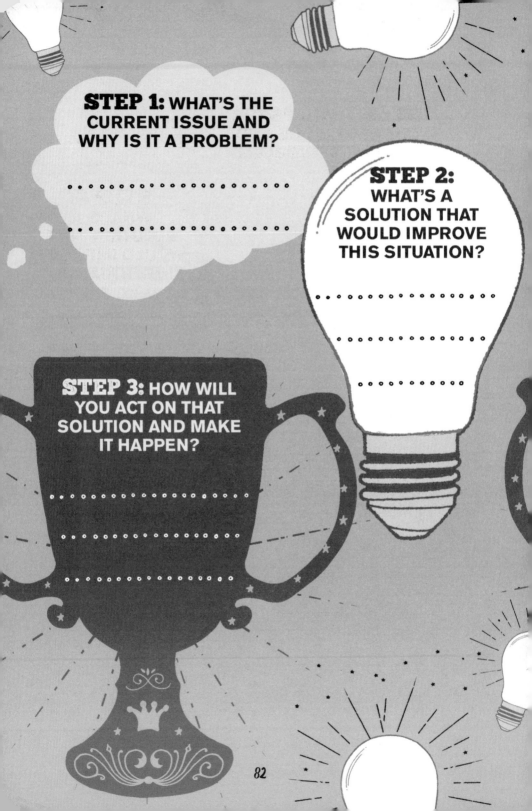

STEP 1: WHAT'S THE CURRENT ISSUE AND WHY IS IT A PROBLEM?

STEP 2: WHAT'S A SOLUTION THAT WOULD IMPROVE THIS SITUATION?

STEP 3: HOW WILL YOU ACT ON THAT SOLUTION AND MAKE IT HAPPEN?

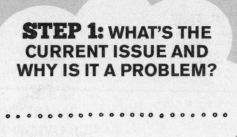

STEP 1: WHAT'S THE CURRENT ISSUE AND WHY IS IT A PROBLEM?

· ·

· ·

STEP 2: WHAT'S A SOLUTION THAT WOULD IMPROVE THIS SITUATION?

· · · · · · · · · · · · · · · · · · ·

· · · · · · · · · · · · · · ·

· · · · · · · · · · · ·

STEP 3: HOW WILL YOU ACT ON THAT SOLUTION AND MAKE IT HAPPEN?

· · · · · · · · · · · · · · · · ·

· · · · · · · · · · · · · · ·

· · · · · · · · · · · · · ·

SOUND LIKE AN ACTION HERO

Negative language can stop us from doing and trying so many brilliant things in life. Often, all we need to do is change the way we look at things. How many times have you said, 'I can't' or 'I'm too busy!' when faced with something difficult?

Try the language of an action hero ...

Here is some hero language for you to ponder:

RATHER THAN SAYING ...   TRY DECLARING ...

I CAN'T   ➡️   I'LL TRY

WHY CAN'T   ➡️   I AM GOING TO
SOMEONE ELSE ...   DO THIS MYSELF

YOU MAKE ME   ➡️   I HAVE CHOSEN TO

IF ONLY I COULD   ➡️   I CAN

Finish the sentences below with things you might have said lately, and then use some action-hero language to turn things around and make everything seem more possible.

I CAN'T...

AN ACTION HERO WOULD SAY:.........................

....

YOU MAKE ME.......................................

AN ACTION HERO WOULD SAY:.........................

....

IF ONLY I COULD...................................

AN ACTION HERO WOULD SAY:.........................

....

SILENCE KID DOUBT

Trying to solve challenges in the world around you is good, but sometimes you need to work on things personal to you, too. And if you're anything like me, the biggest thing holding you back will be **Kid Doubt**, your arch-enemy. Be your own action hero by saying something positive to yourself each day, just as you get out of bed or while you are brushing your teeth. Here are some ideas:

I have great ideas

I am kind

I refuse to quit

SHH!

I can achieve anything

I dare to be ME

I am awesome

You can also help other people to conquer their **Kid Doubt** by saying something kind to them. Compliment them for having a cool idea, their awesome jumper, or for doing something helpful.

SEIZE THE DAY

How many times have you had a great idea, but you've never got around to doing it? Everything else suddenly seems more appealing – even cleaning your room (okay, well maybe not quite that) and so you put off getting on with your great idea. Here are some tips to help you to get going, instead of putting things off day after day.

○ **BREAK IT DOWN.** Divide your project into smaller steps so it seems less overwhelming. Tick off each step on a list once you've completed it. That's very satisfying!

○ **PEER PRESSURE.** Tell other people about your goal so they can check up on you and keep you on track. If you know someone is going to ask how much progress you've made, then you're more likely to be motivated.

○ **BUDDY UP.** Find a friend (or a brother, in my case) with a similar goal; they can help you to stay focused and encourage you to keep going.

○ **CHANGE YOUR ENVIRONMENT.** If it's too noisy or uncomfortable where you are, change your surroundings to help you focus and get rid of distractions.

○ **BE INSPIRED.** Spend time with people who inspire you to take action and stay motivated.

○ **REWARD YOURSELF.** When you've completed a goal, task or reached a deadline, treat yourself! Give yourself a 10-minute break or do something you enjoy.

SEE IT, SOLVE IT!

The best inventions in life are often the ones that make our everyday lives easier. You know the wheelie suitcase? I **ALMOST** invented it. Except, well, **Kid Doubt** got in the way, telling me it was a rubbish idea. Have a think about the things in your life that drive **YOU** bonkers. Is it the toothpaste stuck in the end of the tube and hard to get to? Are your headphone cables always tangling up? Does it drive you crazy when your umbrella turns inside out? Well, now is your chance to have a go at solving your problems, distraction free!

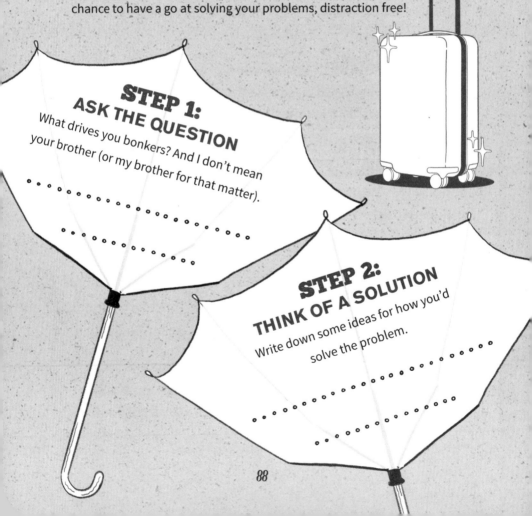

STEP 1:
ASK THE QUESTION
What drives you bonkers? And I don't mean your brother (or my brother for that matter).

STEP 2:
THINK OF A SOLUTION
Write down some ideas for how you'd solve the problem.

STEP 3:
ACT ON IT
Draw your new invention below!

MANIFESTO MAKER

You know, we all come up against problems every day. But, it's how you approach them that determines how big an issue they become. Write your next manifesto point to help you out with your problems in the future.

The next time I come up against a problem in life, I'm going to remember ...

· ·

· ·

When someone is **CRUEL** or acts like a **BULLY**, you don't stoop to their level. **NO,** our motto is, when they go low, **WE GO HIGH.**

Michelle Obama
THE FIRST AFRICAN-AMERICAN
FIRST LADY OF THE USA,
AUTHOR AND ACTIVIST

CONFESSION TIME

As much as we might try, we're not *always* the best versions of ourselves. Occasionally, we may react badly to others because **Kid Doubt** gets involved and we feel hurt, upset or insecure. Now, be totally honest and think about three times that you've been a bit unkind. Perhaps you lost your temper with one of your pals, or maybe one time (or maybe more …) you shouted at your brother for no good reason? Think hard about why you might have had those reactions and how you think you could handle it differently in the future.

I WAS UNKIND TO …

• · ○ · ○ · ○ • · ○ • ○ · ○ ○ ○ · ○ ○ · ○ · ○ · ○ · ○ · ○

I SAID …

• · · · ○ ○ ○ ○ · · · ○ ○ · · · ○ · ○ ○ · ○ ○ · ○ · ○ · ○ ○ ○

I REACTED THIS WAY BECAUSE …

○ · ○ · ○ · ○ · ○ ○ ○ ○ ○ · ○ · ○ · · · ○ ○ · ○ · ○ · ○ ○ ·

IN FUTURE, I'D …

• · ○ · ○ · ○ ○ ○ · ○ · ○ · · ○ · ○ · ○ · ○ · ○ · ○ ○ ○

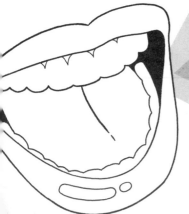

MAKING AMENDS

My mum is one of the kindest people I know, but (and I am ashamed to admit this) I haven't always been as kind to her as I should have been. She once drove 200 miles to drop me off at a table-tennis tournament. When we arrived I realised that I had forgotten my bat. Without hesitation she drove home and got it for me. That day she drove a total of 800 miles! Just for me. And you know what I said to her when she returned? 'Could you not have got back any faster? I'm left with the worst table to practise on now, and it is your fault.' After I said it, I think I could see some tears in her eyes.

I HAVE REGRETTED WHAT I SAID EVER SINCE.

But no one can be perfect all the time. What's important is admitting you've done something wrong, thinking about why you did it and apologising. Sounds easy, right? Oh no, stop right there – apologies can be **REALLY** hard to get right. Here are some tips for next time you need to 'fess up' and admit you did something wrong.

7 STEPS TO A GOOD APOLOGY

1 **Take responsibility.** Even if the other person did something wrong, you need to be responsible for your own actions as well.

2 **Think about why you reacted in that way.** Did you feel upset, defensive or hurt?

3 **How could you make it up to that person?** It can be as simple as saying 'I'm sorry', giving them a hug, or repairing something if you broke it. Think about what you could do to make that person feel better.

4 **If you're struggling with your apology,** role-play or talk it through with someone you trust.

5 **Carry out the apology.** Be honest and make eye contact.

6 **If the person still feels upset,** ask if there's anything else you can do to make it up to them.

7 **Then move on.** Don't let **Kid Doubt** beat you up over a mistake you made and then put right.

KINDNESS CASCADE

When you're kind to people, they are more likely to want to be kind to others too. Before long, loads of people are being kind to each other. It's the gift that keeps on giving! Find three people to be kind to and start your own **KINDNESS CASCADE!** You don't have to do something big – a nice message or a helping hand can be enough.

WHO NEEDS HELP?

....

....

HOW CAN YOU HELP THEM?

....

....

....

HOW ARE YOU GOING TO PUT THIS PLAN INTO ACTION?

....

....

....

WHO COULD YOU DO SOMETHING UNEXPECTEDLY KIND FOR?

....

....

WHAT WILL YOU DO AND WHY?

....

....

WHEN WILL YOU DO IT?

....

....

OU

WHO DID SOMETHING KIND FOR YOU?

....

....

WHAT WILL YOU DO FOR THEM?

....

....

WHEN WILL YOU DO THIS ACT OF KINDNESS?

....

The three people you have just helped just might pass it on ...

DAILY RANDOM ACTS OF KINDNESS

Every November there is an international World Kindness Day, but one day a year hardly seems like enough. I think we should try to be kind every day. One of the most fun ways to be kind is with random acts of kindness. Why don't you try and fill your week with unexpected acts of kindness towards people, places and things.

Fill out this planner. I've put a few ideas in place to get you started . . . .

MONDAY	TUESDAY	WEDNESDAY	THURSDAY	FRIDAY	SATURDAY	SUNDAY
						Offer to help a friend with some tricky homework.

Choose a friend to celebrate for the whole day. It's not their birthday, but at the end of it, they might feel like it was! ✓

Pick up litter on the way to school to help keep your community clean and tidy. ✓

STUDY BUDDIES

What subject do you struggle with at school? And what subject is your favourite? Now, is there anyone in your class you can team up with? Someone who can help you with your tricky subject and who you can help with your best subject? When we help each other, we all win!

A TRICKY SUBJECT FOR ME IS

....

WHO COULD HELP ME IMPROVE?

....

MY BEST SUBJECT IS

....

I COULD HELP

....

BY

....

A *SINGLE ACT* OF **KINDNESS** *throws out* **ROOTS** *in all directions, and the roots* **SPRING UP** *and* **MAKE NEW TREES.**

Amelia Earhart
AVIATION PIONEER

BE KIND TO YOU

BREAK OUT A JIGSAW PUZZLE

With all this helping out of family and friends, you're probably feeling pretty exhausted. I know I am just reading about it! So, it's really important to make sure we look after ourselves, too. Make sure you're taking care of **YOU** by choosing some of these relaxing activities to help you unwind.

Go for a bike ride

CUDDLE UP AND WATCH A MOVIE

ADD TO A SCRAPBOOK (OR YOUR ACHIEVEMENT ALBUM?)

LISTEN TO AN AUDIOBOOK

Take silly pictures with your family or a group of friends

HAVE A BATH

DRAW, PAINT OR CRAFT

LISTEN TO MUSIC

Have a warm drink

TAKE A NAP

SPEND SOME TIME IN THE GARDEN OR IN YOUR LOCAL PARK, LISTENING TO NATURE

BAKE OR COOK A MEAL

Go for a walk or a run

BUILD A FORT WITH THE CUSHIONS FROM YOUR SOFA AND PLAY A GAME OR READ A BOOK INSIDE IT

MANIFESTO MAKER

It's **COOL TO BE KIND** (and there can never be too much kindness in the world) so it's time to add this to your manifesto.

The next time I feel like being unkind, I'm going to remember ...

★ •

• •

I wouldn't have **GROWN** if I hadn't **FALLEN** and stumbled and gotten **BACK UP.**

Lewis Hamilton
DARING-TO-FAIL
FORMULA 1 DRIVER

BUMPS IN THE ROAD

THE PATH TO SUCCESS

It's a fact of life that life is not always easy. Even if you study really hard for a test, sometimes **Kid Doubt** shows up on the day and makes you forget everything you have learned. Or you plan a great outdoor birthday party and it rains. Or you love your house and your friends, but you have to move because your dad gets a new job. Whether it's a big or a small thing, life can throw us curveballs. How you handle them is what makes all the difference.

OFTEN, WE MAKE A PLAN AND WE THINK IT'LL GO LIKE THIS:

WHEN REALLY, IT LOOKS MORE LIKE THIS:

These two lines both have the same start and end point – one just takes a bit longer to get to the end than the other. The first line is often how we think a plan will go, and the second line is often how the plan turns out. But what's important is that both of these lines still finish in the same place; one just has a few more bumps in the road and may take a little bit longer. These bumps aren't a complete disaster, though. It's completely natural to feel upset when things don't work out how we expected, but it's how we move forwards from those upsets that's important.

THERE ARE BOUND TO BE BUMPS ALONG THE WAY. IF WE KNOW THAT IN ADVANCE, IT WON'T BE SUCH A SHOCK WHEN THEY HAPPEN.

SHOCK ABSORBERS

One of the best ways to cope with life's roller coaster is to be prepared, and limit the unexpected by planning. Below are some 'shocks' you might face in life. I've come up with some suggestions on how to deal with them, but can you add some more of your own?

SHOCK!

You pressed snooze too many times and overslept your alarm on the day of a big test.

Shock absorber

Don't panic! Take a deep breath, focus on getting dressed and to school as quickly as possible. In future, go to bed earlier so you're less tired, and ask someone else in the house to make sure you're up on time.

SHOCK!

You did not do as well in an exam as you expected, and feel nervous about telling your parents.

Shock absorber

First, take a deep breath and do speak to your parents. They will want to help you through this! You could also talk to your teacher about the result, and find out which areas you may need more help with. We can learn from failure and turn things around!

SHOCK!

You forgot your mum's birthday.

Shock absorber

Be honest. Let your mum know you love her and admit that you forgot. But come up with a way to make it up to her and follow through with your plan. Then set a reminder in your phone or on a calendar for next year (two years in a row could be unforgiveable).

SHOCK!

Shock absorber

SHOCK!

Shock absorber

STICK OR TWIST?

Stick or twist? You might be asked this if you are playing a card game. Stick means, 'I'm happy with what I have', while twist means, 'I might just be happier with a different card, so I'll risk it and swap'. There is a long-standing card-game dispute in the Syed family. My brother took a risk. He went with twist, got a bad card and lost the game. In anger, he said that he was in fact asking for a Twix (honestly, I know …).

Sometimes you start down one path and you hit a bump in the road. Do you find a way to get over the **bump** and **stick** with what you have, or **twist** and try something different altogether?

BUMP IN THE ROAD

You've wanted to be in a band for ages, so you start playing the guitar. You get really shy about playing in front of everyone else and think this might actually ruin your plans of joining a band. Do you stick or twist?

STICK?

It can be hard to keep going with something. A good test is to ask yourself if it's making you happy. If playing the guitar gets a big tick, then keep doing it! But break down where you want to get to into small pieces. Rather than walking onto a stage in front of hundreds of people for your first show, start small. Play in front of one person you trust and build confidence from there. The point is to start small, and practise until you are ready to move on to something bigger.

TWIST?

If you realise that playing the guitar just isn't for you, that's okay. We're allowed to try things and change our mind – as long as you're not giving up just because you weren't instantly brilliant. If you still long to join a band, why not try the drums instead?

Now it's your turn. Think of a bump in the road you're facing, and ask yourself whether you should stick with it, or twist and change direction.

WHAT'S THE BUMP IN THE ROAD?

. . . .

. . . .

STICK?

. . . .

. . . .

TWIST?

. . . .

. . . .

THE RESILIENCE:
A BRAND-NEW BAND

When you're facing a challenge, you don't have to deal with it alone. Talking to someone you trust can really help you feel better, and they may have great ideas on how to fix things. So, think about who you could enlist as your 'Resilience Roadies' – the people at school, at home, or in your community – who you can go to for help.

THE MANAGER

They help you see the bigger picture.

NAME: ....

WHY THEY ARE A GOOD FIT FOR THE JOB:

....

THE SOUND ENGINEER

They encourage you to talk yourself up.

NAME: ....

WHY THEY ARE A GOOD FIT FOR THE JOB:

....

THE BACKING SINGERS

They always support you, no matter what.

NAME: ....

WHY THEY ARE A GOOD FIT FOR THE JOB:

....

THE CO-WRITER

The person who helps you brainstorm ideas when you're stuck.

NAME: ....

WHY THEY ARE A GOOD FIT FOR THE JOB:

....

THE SECURITY

When things get a little too much to handle, they step in to help.

NAME: ....

WHY THEY ARE A GOOD FIT FOR THE JOB:

....

BUMP OR ROADBLOCK?

Everyone reacts to situations differently. Some people can brush things off and keep moving forwards, some people take mistakes really hard and get stopped in their tracks, whilst others learn to keep going, even when it's tricky. Take this quiz and find out how **YOU** deal with bumps in the road.

1 **You and your family were watching the news, and you saw something that scared you. What's your reaction?**

A. You pretend you didn't see it and ignore your worried thoughts.

B. You hide under your bed and refuse to come out. The world is a scary place.

C. You talk to an adult you trust about how it made you feel.

2 **You studied really hard for your science exam, but you didn't get the grade you were hoping for. What do you do next?**

A. Put the test in the bin and pretend you're not bothered about science.

B. Get really upset and plan to never ever study for a test again. What's the point?

C. Ask someone who got a better mark to help you study for the next test. You tried really hard, but to keep improving you're going to need some outside help.

3 Someone in your class is having a birthday party, and lots of your friends have been given an invite – but you haven't. How do you behave?

A. You decide to ignore that person. Who cares? You're fine without friends anyway.

B. You lock yourself in the bathroom and refuse to talk to anyone about why you're so upset.

C. You go home and talk to your parents; you're sad and confused so you decide to get some help about what to do.

4 You've baked some treats for your class, but trip over the cat and drop the box on the floor. The cakes are ruined. What will you do?

A. Put them in the bin and don't tell anyone about it.

B. Refuse to go to school until you've baked some more. You're worried no one will like you if you turn up empty-handed.

C. Laugh! Accidents happen. And ask your parents if you can buy something from the shops to give your class instead.

5 You've just finished a history project that you're really proud of, but the computer crashes and you lose all your work. How do you react?

A. You don't send in your homework that night. You go to bed and decide to deal with whatever consequences come your way tomorrow.

B. You stay up worrying all night and refuse to go to school the next day. You can't face not handing in your project.

C. You ask someone to help you redo as much as possible, then explain what happened to the teacher the next day and ask if they'll give you a bit more time.

6 You've just come back from a friend's house to find out your brother has broken your new birthday present. What do you say to your brother?

A. Nothing, you ignore him completely.

B. You shout at him over and over. It was only your birthday last week, it was brand-new!

C. You're upset, but you ask him to explain what happened. You know he (probably) didn't do it on purpose.

MOSTLY As

You're good at moving on, but you're not always honest with yourself about how these mishaps make you feel. Keep moving forwards, but remember it's okay to ask for help and let others know that you care about the things you do.

MOSTLY Bs

You can find things pretty overwhelming and find it quite tricky to see the positives in moving forwards. Try not to be so hard on yourself, and surround yourself with people who are good at helping you deal with bumps in the road.

MOSTLY Cs

You're really good at bouncing back from tricky situations. Keep up the good work and remember there's always something to be learned from the times things don't go to plan. The tips in this chapter will help you learn how to bounce back – just keep working at it!

BOUNCE-BACK TIPS

Sometimes, dusting yourself off after a disappointment can be easier said than done. But, here are some tips for **BOUNCING BACK**. Now, it is fair to say that I followed none of the tips below when I crashed out of the Sydney Olympics. Instead, I booked the first flight home. But trust me, I would have felt a lot better if I had followed the tips below. Sigh.

1 **Take a deep breath and count to ten or twenty, or thirty!** Take as long as you need to feel calmer. When we stop and take a moment to breathe, we soon realise it's not quite as bad as we first thought.

2 **Talk to a friend, family member or a teacher.** If you're doubting yourself, asking someone else to remind you of all the things you're great at can really help to reassure you.

3 **Go to your Achievement Album.** Looking at all of the other brilliant things you've achieved will make you realise how resilient you are.

4 **Get a good night's sleep.** Everything can feel much worse when we're tired.

5 **Get some exercise.** This will help you ease your frustration and look at the situation more calmly. Try going for a walk.

 What would you do to bounce back from the problems shown on the opposite page? Add some of your own examples and write down which of the tips would have helped you face these problems a bit easier.

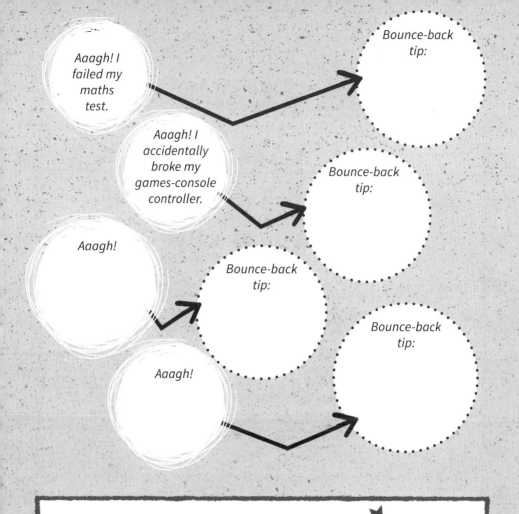

Aaagh! I failed my maths test.

Aaagh! I accidentally broke my games-console controller.

Aaagh!

Aaagh!

Bounce-back tip:

Bounce-back tip:

Bounce-back tip:

Bounce-back tip:

MANIFESTO MAKER

It's time to pull together all the resilience tips you've learnt in this chapter for your manifesto.

The next time something doesn't go to plan, I'm going to remember ...

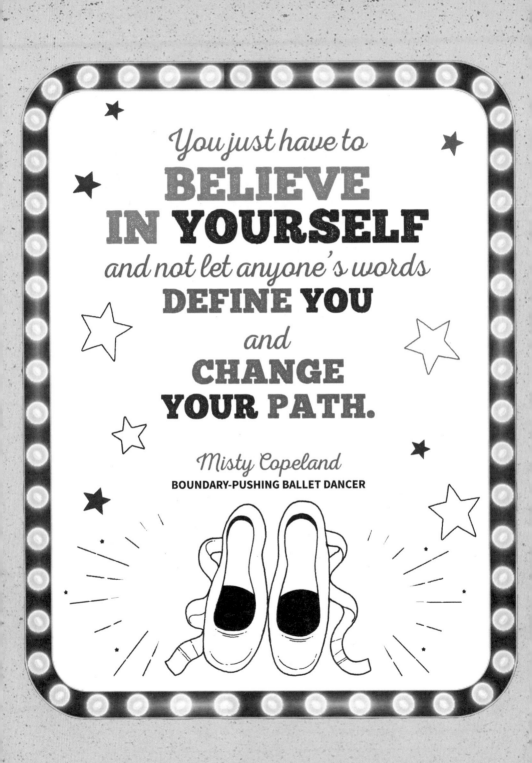

You just have to
**BELIEVE
IN YOURSELF**
and not let anyone's words
DEFINE YOU
and
**CHANGE
YOUR PATH.**

Misty Copeland
BOUNDARY-PUSHING BALLET DANCER

FOLLOW YOUR OWN PATH

THIS WAY

THAT WAY

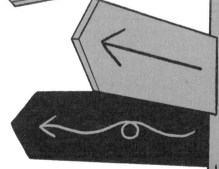

BEING **ME**

With each year that passes you collect experiences: you've tried more things, overcome more hurdles and you know yourself a little bit better. And the more we get to know ourselves, the better we become at working out when something's right for us, or if it's best left to other people.

I STARTED TO TALK

I IGNORED KID DOUBT WHEN ...

....

....

I WAS BORN

MY FIRST DAY OF SCHOOL

Fill in this timeline of your life so far and think of the times when someone suggested you did or tried something, but you knew it wasn't right for you, so you stuck to your own path. Maybe everyone was signing up for running club, but drama club was more your thing?

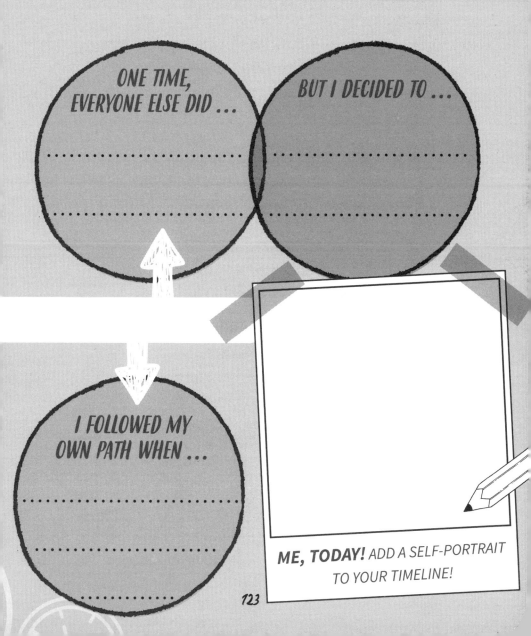

ONE TIME,
EVERYONE ELSE DID ...

· · · · · · · · · · · · · · · · · · · ·

· · · · · · · · · · · · · · · · · · · ·

BUT I DECIDED TO ...

· · · · · · · · · · · · · · · · · · · ·

· · · · · · · · · · · · · · · · · · · ·

I FOLLOWED MY
OWN PATH WHEN ...

· · · · · · · · · · · · · · · · · · · ·

· · · · · · · · · · · · · · · · · · · ·

· · · · · · · · · · · · ·

ME, TODAY! *ADD A SELF-PORTRAIT TO YOUR TIMELINE!*

WHAT'S YOUR PATH?

Working out 'who you are' and where you want to go in life can be a pretty daunting task. The best place to start is by figuring out what's **IMPORTANT** in your life and what makes you **HAPPY**. Look at each area in your life below. Tick which sentence you think fits you best to help you work out which things are important to you ...

FRIENDS

1 **When it comes to friends, would you rather:**
- O Be surrounded by a big group of friends ☐
- O Have one or two really close friends ☐

2 **Would you rather your friends:**
- O Keep pushing you outside of your comfort zone ☐
- O Support and encourage you in your interests ☐

3 **Do you like to:**
- O See and speak to your friends every day ☐
- O Have a bit of alone time, knowing they'll be ready to hang out again when you are ☐

What have you learned about yourself and your friendship groups?

. . . .

. . . .

FAMILY

1 **When it comes to family, do you feel that:**

O They're your closest friends. ☐

O They drive you mad, but you know they're always ☐
there for you.

2 **At the weekend, you would rather:**

O Hang out with your family ☐

O You love your family, but you need some time ☐
alone after a busy week

O Spend more time with your friends, your family ☐
understand you need to hang out together

3 **In your family, you're:**

O The funny one ☐

O The helpful one ☐

O The quiet one ☐

O The sensible one ☐

O The artistic one ☐

O The book-smart one ☐

What have you found out about yourself and how you
behave within your family?

. . . .

. . . .

Ha

Hahaha

Haha

SCHOOL

1 **At school:**
- ○ You're always really focused in the mornings ☐
- ○ It takes you a while to get going, the afternoon is your best time of day ☐

2 **When you're set homework:**
- ○ You like to get it done and out of the way as soon as possible ☐
- ○ You're always a night-before kind of student ☐

3 **When it comes to lessons, you prefer:**
- ○ Group activities where you can work on a problem as part of a team ☐
- ○ Quiet study, when you can concentrate and work through a problem alone ☐

What have you learned about your approach to school?

....

....

HOBBIES

(1) **When it comes to hobbies, you:**
- O Focus on just one thing until you're really good at it ☐
- O Prefer to do loads of different things at once ☐

(2) **You like your hobbies to be:**
- O Something you can do by yourself ☐
- O Part of a team effort ☐

(3) **With your hobby:**
- O You have an exact plan of how you're going to improve at each step ☐
- O You just go with the flow and see where it takes you ☐

When it comes to hobbies, what type of person are you?

· ·

· ·

CHOICES, CHOICES, CHOICES

Now you know what matters to you, you'll want to move closer to your goals. But while some things we do in life move us **CLOSER** to our goals, other things move us **FURTHER** away. Try spotting the things in your life that are either helping or hindering your success.

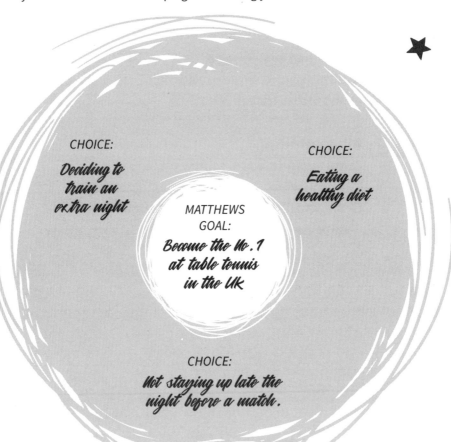

CHOICE:

Deciding to train an extra night

MATTHEWS GOAL:

Become the No.1 at table tennis in the Uk

CHOICE:

Eating a healthy diet

CHOICE:

Not staying up late the night before a match.

Write down some of your goals in the middle of this circle. They might be learning a new skill or taking more time for yourself. Next, fill in the choices that you've made lately to help you achieve your goals. Finally, identify if these things have helped you get closer or further away from where you wanted to be. I've filled in my 'choice circle' to help get you started.

CHOICE:

CHOICE:

GOAL:

CHOICE:

CHOICE:

MATTHEW'S MANIFESTO

If you've read *Dare to Be You* then you'll know that I like to have a plan. Something to keep me on my path. It helps when I get a bit unsure, or **Kid Doubt** decides to rock up. Take a little look at my plan, below.

1 **Make friends with people who like you for YOU.**

Make friends with people who will build you up, not knock you down. If you think there aren't many of those around, then you are looking in the wrong places.

2 **Make choices based on what you feel is right, for YOU.**

There are so many choices and decisions to be made – all the time. Make these based on what YOU would like for yourself, based on the values that YOU feel are important.

3 **Don't blindly copy other people. Be YOU.**

Pick out the traits in others that you REALLY admire and copy those. Don't feel the need to copy things that really won't help you achieve your goals or to be true to yourself.

Don't be afraid to do things at YOUR own pace.

Be brave. Ask to slow down if you need to. Everyone learns in different ways.

 YOU should be prepared to be flexible.

You might not find your own path straight away, and that is fine. You might need to change it up a few times before you find what really works for you.

 Be kind. And don't listen to anyone who isn't kind to YOU.

Kindness really pays off. There are major benefits to being kind, so don't underestimate its power!

MANIFESTO MAKER

You know those 'things to remember when ...' that you've been noting down throughout the book? Now it's time to pull them together and build your own manifesto. First you need to create your final one ...

When I want to follow my own path, I am going to remember ...

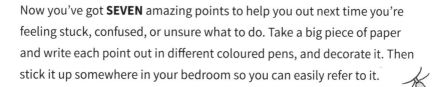

Now you've got **SEVEN** amazing points to help you out next time you're feeling stuck, confused, or unsure what to do. Take a big piece of paper and write each point out in different coloured pens, and decorate it. Then stick it up somewhere in your bedroom so you can easily refer to it.

CONCLUSION

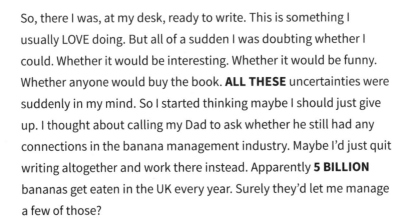

Do you want the good news or the bad news?

The bad news is that I had a visit from my
Kid Doubt while sitting down to write this
conclusion. Out of nowhere. I hadn't seen him in
a long while and so I wasn't entirely pleased when
he and his grey face turned up laughing at me every
time I tried to put some words on paper. And as usual,
whenever he is around, I begin to worry and become a little
less sure of myself.

So, there I was, at my desk, ready to write. This is something I
usually LOVE doing. But all of a sudden I was doubting whether I
could. Whether it would be interesting. Whether it would be funny.
Whether anyone would buy the book. **ALL THESE** uncertainties were
suddenly in my mind. So I started thinking maybe I should just give
up. I thought about calling my Dad to ask whether he still had any
connections in the banana management industry. Maybe I'd just quit
writing altogether and work there instead. Apparently **5 BILLION**
bananas get eaten in the UK every year. Surely they'd let me manage
a few of those?

I was in a banana-flavoured spiral of DOUBT. And **Kid Doubt** loved it.

But ... do you want the good news now? I took a deep breath and I
remembered the plan.

THE PLAN. My Manifesto.

The one that I have used ever since I almost
burnt the local bakery down trying to impress
some of my brother's friends (you've read *Dare To
Be You* now right, so you know all about that seriously bad move?).
The one I have used every single time I have felt unsure, or like I didn't
fit in, or like things were not going as well as I had hoped. And it hasn't
let me down yet.

And there is even better news ... you're one step ahead. You've got
as far as here already! Which means that even if you haven't done all
of the activities in this journal, you've made a start. You've thought
about your own **Kid Doubt** and devised strategies to keep him or
her quiet. You've thought about your goals and how you're going to
achieve them. You've thought about what makes you different and
why that means you are brilliant.

YOU HAVE STARTED MAKING YOUR OWN PLAN.

Once I had remembered my plan I knew that I should leave the
5 billion bananas to the professional banana managers and focus
on writing. Which is what I truly love.

And since I decided that, I haven't seen **Kid Doubt's** miserable
face again.

But, do you know what? He'll be back. Maybe not for ages and maybe not very often. But everyone has a **Kid Doubt** no matter who they are. And from time to time **Kid Doubt** will be there, causing anxiety, causing worries, causing us to question ourselves.

But if we remember the plan, we'll be able to deal with **Kid Doubt** build our confidence and be ready to face the challenges ahead.

So, remember ...

- O Make friends with people who like you for being YOU
- O Make choices based on what you feel is right for YOU
- O Don't blindly copy other people
- O Ask questions, see whether there is something out there that might work better for YOU
- O Don't be afraid to do things at your own pace
- O Be prepared to be flexible and do things differently if something changes
- O Be kind. Its better for everyone

And also remember to eat 100 bananas (probably not in one go). How else are we going to make it to 5 billion between us?

But whatever happens, be proud of who you are. Be proud of the things you have achieved. Be proud of the goals that you have chosen to work towards. You Are Awesome.

SO...

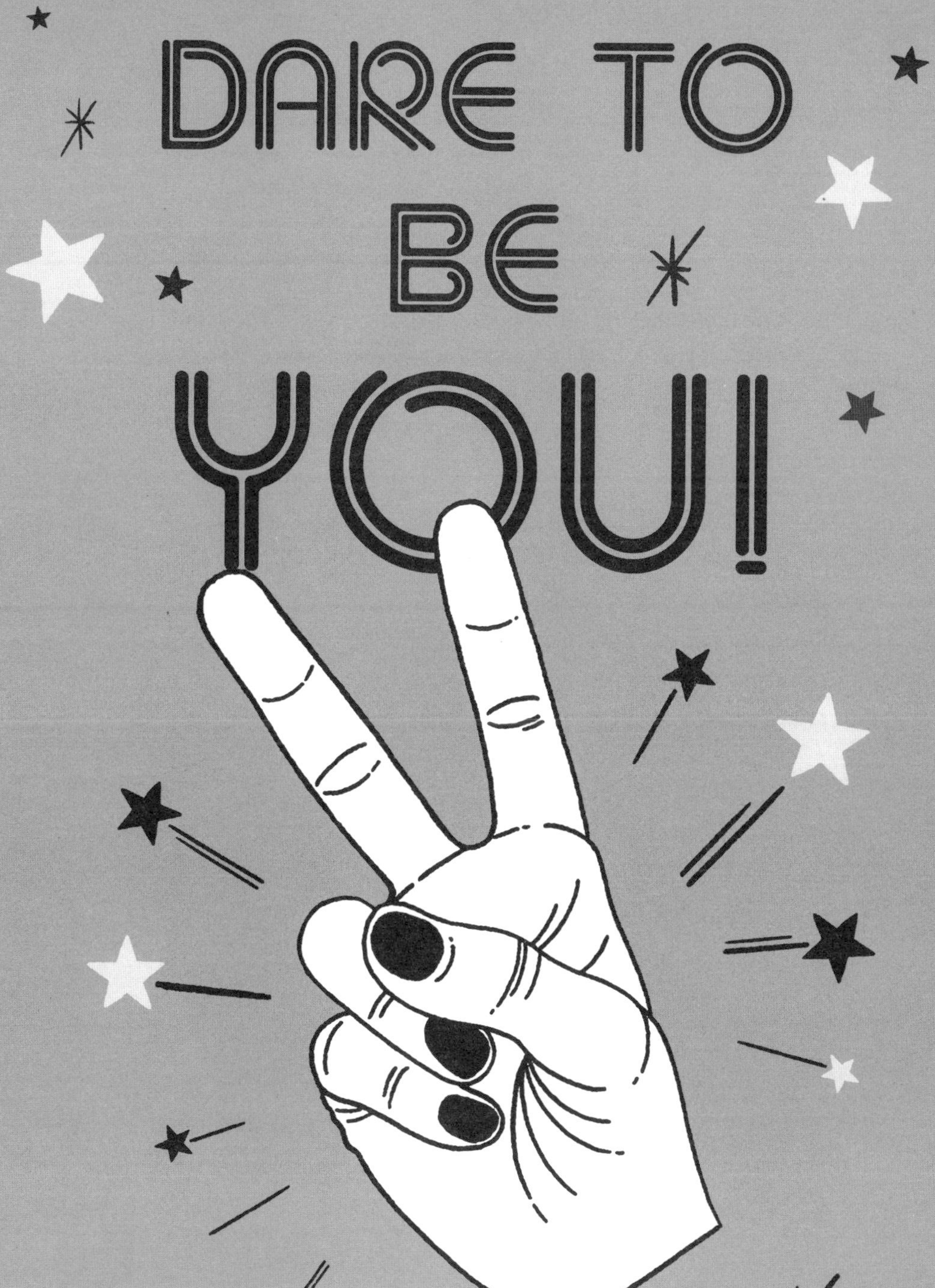
DARE TO
BE
YOU!

Find out **WHO YOU ARE.** And **DO IT** on purpose

Dolly Parton,
SINGER, PHILANTHROPIST
AND DARING ORIGINAL

MY DARING TO BE ME NOTES

_____

_____

_____

_____

_____

_____

_____

_____

_____

MY DARING TO BE ME NOTES

_____

_____

_____

_____

_____

_____

_____

_____

_____

Discover more AWESOME

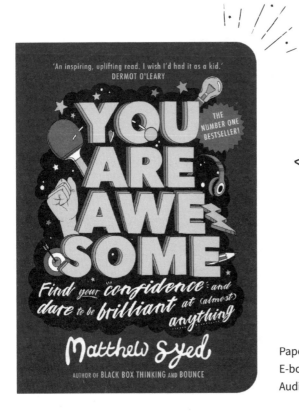

Paperback | 978 1 5263 6115 8
E-book | 978 1 5263 6133 2
Audio book | 978 1 5263 6157 8

YOU ARE AWESOME

"I'm no good at sport … " "I can't do maths… " Sound familiar? If you believe you can't do something, chances are you won't try. But what if you really could get better at maths or sport? What if you could excel at anything you put your mind to? This inspiring guide empowers young readers to find the confidence to realise their potential with a positive growth mindset.

books by Matthew Syed!

Paperback | 978 1 5263 6166 0

THE YOU ARE AWESOME JOURNAL

Find your way to awesome with this brilliant toolkit of goals, plans and challenges that gives kids the confidence to come up with their own plan of action. Whether setting out their goals, planning the best practice ever or keeping calm with breathing exercises, this is the perfect journal for anyone who dreams big – and who wants to make those dreams come true.

From the bestselling author of
YOU ARE AWESOME

Dare
TO BE
YOU

Defy self-doubt, fearlessly
follow your own path
and be confidently you!

Matthew Syed

Paperback | 978 1 5263 6237 7
E-Book | 978 1 5263 6238 4
Audio book | 978 1 5263 6239 1

DARE TO BE YOU

Drawing examples from sport, science and even business, *Dare to Be You* empowers young readers to follow their own path, love what makes them different and question the world around them. With a mix of hilarious text, stylish illustration, personal insights and inspiring real-life examples, including Greta Thunberg and Malala Yousafzai, Matthew Syed introduces children to the power of diverse thinking.

REFERENCES

WILL SMITH – Smith, Will. *Journal Times*, 13 July 2004 (spoken statement). https://journaltimes.com/news/national/article_4323eaf6-a8c2-54c6-97b8-3273e5a70cbe.html, accessed 28th October 2020.

OPRAH WINFREY – Winfrey, Oprah. The Oprah Winfrey Show Finale, 25 May 2011. (spoken statement) http://www.oprah.com/oprahshow/the-oprah-winfrey-show-finale_1/6, accessed 28 October 2020.

VENUS WILLIAMS – Williams, Venus. *Bustle*, 9th April 2015. https://www.bustle.com/articles/109299-7-extraordinary-venus-williams-quotes-that-prove-shes-a-force-to-be-reckoned-with, accessed 28 October 2020.

EMMA STONE – Stone, Emma. MTV acceptance speech. http://www.mtv.com/news/1686420/trailblazer-emma-stone-mtv-movie-awards/

TAYLOR SWIFT – Swift, Taylor. *Twitter.com*, 6 May 2014. (written statement) https://twitter.com/QuoteTaySwift/status/463467946984345600, accessed 28 October 2020.

LIZZO – Lizzo. *Instagram.com*, 10 December 2019. (spoken statement) https://www.instagram.com/p/B54DQylhlOY/, accessed 28 October 2020.

ELLEN MACARTHUR – MacArthur, Dame Ellen. 'The surprising thing I learned sailing solo around the world.' *Ted.com*, March 2015. (spoken statement) https://www.ted.com/talks/dame_ellen_macarthur_the_surprising_thing_i_learned_sailing_solo_around_the_world/transcript, accessed 28 October 2020.

STEVE JOBS – Jobs, Steve. Commencement Address at Stanford University, 12 June 2005. https://www.americanrhetoric.com/speeches/stevejobsstanfordcommencement.htm, accessed 2 November, 2020.

BARACK OBAMA – Obama, Barack. 'Barack Obama's Feb. 5 Speech', *The New York Times/Federal News Service*, 5 February 2008. https://www.nytimes.com/2008/02/05/us/politics/05text-obama.html, accessed 28 October 2020.

MICHELLE OBAMA – Obama, Michelle. Speech at the Democratic National Convention, 25 July 2016. (reported statement). https://www.oxfordreference.com/view/10.1093/acref/9780191843730.001.0001/q-oro-ed5-00016286, accessed 28 October 2020.

AMELIA EARHART – Earhart, Amelia. (reported statement.) https://www.ameliaearhart.com/quotes/, accessed 28 October 2020.

LEWIS HAMILTON – Hamilton, Lewis. 'I want to make amends.' *GQ Magazine,* 26 August 2018. (https://www.gq-magazine.co.uk/article/lewis-hamilton-interview-2018, accessed 28 October 2020.

MISTY COPELAND – Copeland, Misty. 'Ballet Saved Misty Copeland From Middle School Misery'. *Elle Magazine*, 19 September 2016. https://www.elle.com/culture/interviews/a39099/misty-copeland-marley-mag-interview/, accessed 29 October 2020

DOLLY PARTON - Parton, Dolly. *Twitter.com*, 20 July 2009. (written statement) https://twitter.com/DollyParton/status/2740290248, accessed 29 October 2020.